It's Sunday—the day of the Lord!

All over the world, bells are ringing from church steeples, calling people to Mass.

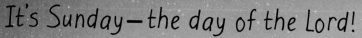

Young people and old people,
rich people and poor people,
sad people and happy people,
people from around the world.
We are all members of God's family ...

... and we as Catholics gather together
to praise and thank God at Mass!

We begin by joining all our voices together in song to make one beautiful sound.

The priest and other ministers process to the front of the church led by the cross and candles. This reminds us that we are all brothers and sisters who are led by the love and light of Jesus.

INTRODUCTORY RITES
The Sign of the Cross & Greeting

We make the Sign of the Cross together.

The priest says,
**"In the name of the Father,
and of the Son,
and of the Holy Spirit."**

We say, **"Amen."**

The priest greets us with a very old greeting:
"The Lord be with you."

And we answer all together,
"And with your spirit."

We say that we are sorry for the times when we have not acted like friends of Jesus.

Lord, have mercy.
Lord, have mercy.

Christ, have mercy.
Christ, have mercy.

Lord, have mercy.
Lord, have mercy.

INTRODUCTORY RITES
The Gloria

We sing our praise to God just as the angels did when Jesus was born.

Glory to God in the highest,
and on earth peace to people of good will.
We praise you, we bless you, we adore you, we glorify you,
we give you thanks for your great glory...

It's time to sit down. We listen better when we are sitting, and we want to listen because God is going to speak to us! Yes, it is God we hear when the readers proclaim the Holy Scriptures to us.

The **First Reading** is usually from the oldest part of the Bible. When we listen to this reading, it is like hearing a story about our great-great-great-great-grandparents in faith.

When the reading is finished, the reader says, "The word of the Lord." We are grateful that God has spoken to us, so we exclaim, "Thanks be to God."

After the **First Reading**, we sing the Psalm. Psalms are very old song-prayers from the Bible. The cantor usually sings the verses and we sing the response.

In the **Second Reading**, we hear the first followers of Jesus tell us about God's great love.

Again the reader reminds us that God has spoken to us, saying,
"The word of the Lord."
Again we exclaim, "**Thanks be to God.**"

Now we are about to listen to the greatest story of all—a story about Jesus. It is called the **Gospel**, which means Good News. There are four Gospels. They were written by Saint Matthew, Saint Mark, Saint Luke and Saint John.

Because the Gospel stories are so important to us, we stand up to listen. We want to shout, "Hooray! Praise God!" We have a very old word that means "Praise God!" We sing this word while the priest or deacon carries the Book of Gospels to the place where the Gospel will be proclaimed. That word is **Alleluia!**

There is one time of the year when we don't sing this wonderful, joyful Alleluia! Do you know when that is? During Lent. For those 40 days, our **Gospel Acclamation** changes. Many churches sing **Praise to you, Lord Jesus Christ, King of endless glory!**

Before he reads the Gospel, the priest or deacon says, **"The Lord be with you."** We say, **"And with your spirit."**

Then he says, **"A reading from the holy Gospel according to..."** And we reply, **"Glory to you, O Lord."**

While we say this, we make a little cross on our forehead so we will understand God's word, on our lips so we will speak God's word, and on our heart so we will love God's word.

When the priest or deacon is finished, he says, **"The Gospel of the Lord."** We reply, **"Praise to you, Lord Jesus Christ."**

The Bible was written thousands of years ago. Sometimes the words and the message are hard for us to understand. The priest or deacon explains the readings to help us understand what God is saying to us today. This is called the **Homily**.

After we listen to God's word, we tell the world what we believe! We call this the Profession of Faith. This is also called the **Creed**.

I believe in God, the Father almighty, Creator of heaven and earth,
and in Jesus Christ, his only Son, our Lord,
who was conceived by the Holy Spirit,
born of the Virgin Mary,
suffered under Pontius Pilate, was crucified, died and was buried;
he descended into hell;
on the third day he rose again from the dead;
he ascended into heaven,
and is seated at the right hand of God the Father almighty;
from there he will come to judge the living and the dead.
I believe in the Holy Spirit,
the holy catholic Church, the communion of saints,
the forgiveness of sins, the resurrection of the body, and life everlasting.
Amen.

In the **Prayer of the Faithful**, we bring all our hopes and dreams and worries to God. We pray for the **Church** and the **world**. We pray for **people in need**. We pray for our own **community**. We pray for those who are **sick** and those we love who have **died**.

The prayers usually end with "... **we pray to the Lord.**"

We respond, "**Lord, hear our prayer.**"

Sometimes we are invited to share our own private prayers with God. What would you like to pray for?

After we offer our prayers to God, we offer our gifts.

Bread and wine are presented to the priest. As we offer the bread and wine, we also offer our hearts and lives to God.

Soon after, we ask God to make this bread and wine holy.
We ask God to make US holy, too!

We offer a great prayer of praise and thanksgiving to God. It is called the **Eucharistic Prayer**.

The priest begins by saying (or singing):
"The Lord be with you."
We reply, **"And with your spirit."**

"Lift up your hearts."
"We lift them up to the Lord."

"Let us give thanks to the Lord our God."
"It is right and just."

Then we join with all the angels in heaven and sing a song of praise to God.

Holy, Holy, Holy Lord God of hosts.
Heaven and earth are full of your glory.
Hosanna in the highest.
Blessed is he who comes in the name of the Lord.
Hosanna in the highest.

At this holy moment, the priest asks God the Father to send the Holy Spirit to change our gifts of bread and wine into the Body and Blood of Jesus. The priest retells the story of Jesus' last meal with his friends.

We pray with all the saints for the Pope and the Church, and we pray for our family and friends.
Jesus, the Son of God, is God the Father's perfect gift to us, so we make our thanksgiving gift back to God the Father.

Together we proclaim the mystery of our faith by saying one of these prayers:

We proclaim your Death, O Lord, and profess your Resurrection until you come again.

or

When we eat this Bread and drink this Cup, we proclaim your Death, O Lord, until you come again.

or

Save us, Saviour of the world, for by your Cross and Resurrection, you have set us free.

Then the priest praises God.

When we are finished the prayer, everyone sings a loud and joyful "Amen."

We pray together the prayer that Jesus taught.
This is a prayer that we should all know by heart.

Our Father, who art in heaven,
hallowed be thy name;
thy kingdom come,
thy will be done
on earth as it is in heaven.
Give us this day our daily bread,
and forgive us our trespasses,
as we forgive those who trespass against us;
and lead us not into temptation,
but deliver us from evil. Amen.

When the prayer is finished, the priest asks
God to keep us safe and free from worries
until Jesus returns. We answer,

"For the kingdom, the power and the glory
are yours now and for ever. Amen."

We know that we must live in peace if we are to be true friends of Jesus and each other.

The priest says to us, **"The peace of the Lord be with you always."**

We reply, **"And with your spirit."**

Then we offer a Sign of Peace to one another by turning to the people near us and saying, **"Peace be with you."**

Now the priest does what Jesus did at the Last Supper. He prays over the Sacred Offerings, which are now the Body and Blood of Jesus.

And then we sing or say:

Lamb of God, you take away the sins of the world, have mercy on us.

Lamb of God, you take away the sins of the world, have mercy on us.

Lamb of God, you take away the sins of the world grant us peace.

The priest holds up the Host and proclaims what it has become:

"Behold the Lamb of God, behold him who takes away the sins of the world. Blessed are those called to the supper of the Lamb."

The Host looks like bread, but it is now the Body of Jesus. The chalice holds what looks like wine, but it is now the Precious Blood of Jesus.

We answer with words that remind us of the Roman soldier who asked Jesus to heal his servant:

"Lord, I am not worthy that you should enter under my roof, but only say the word and my soul shall be healed."

At **Communion**, Catholics come forward to receive Jesus in the Holy Eucharist.

The priest holds up the Host and says, **"The Body of Christ."**

We answer, **"Amen."**

Sometimes the minister offers the chalice of wine and says, **"The Blood of Christ."**

Again we answer, **"Amen."**

We return to our seats, where we sing the Communion hymn and give thanks to Jesus for coming into our hearts.

When we celebrate our First Eucharist, we share fully in this wonderful sacrament for the first time.

Finally, we are sent forth to do God's work in the world.

The priest says, **"The Lord be with you."**
We reply, **"And with your spirit."**

We make the Sign of the Cross while the priest gives us the **Final Blessing**:
"May almighty God bless you, the Father, and the Son, and the Holy Spirit."

We say, **"Amen."**

Now WE must become the Body of Christ in the world.
WE must be Jesus' hands reaching out to others.
WE must be Jesus' heart bringing God's love to the world.

CONCLUDING RITES
The Dismissal

The Mass is over!
We are dismissed with the words
"Go in peace."

We exclaim, **"Thanks be to God."**

We sing a joyful song and go forth!

We are ready to bring to the world the Good News
we have heard and seen and touched!

Dear Parents and Caregivers

Helping your children learn to love the Lord's Day!

To make Sundays a positive experience for the whole family, try these tips.

- **Come to Mass every Sunday.** Children love and need routine. If they know Sunday is church day, they accept that as fact. Attending now and then leads children to see church as optional, making them more likely to protest.

- **...even when on vacation.** When we take our children to Mass when travelling, we teach them that they are part of a Universal Church and have a spiritual home in every town and country! While celebrating the similarities, discuss the differences in language, architecture, music and local customs.

- **Sit up front.** Children behave better when they are closer to the action, so sit near the sanctuary or the choir. Don't worry about being a distraction: Jesus welcomed children, and so should his followers.

- **Encourage participation in word, song and action.** Teach children the simplest responses and gestures as early as possible so these become second nature.

- **Discuss the readings.** Have a conversation in the car or at the Sunday dinner table about the readings or the homily.

- **Make a "church kit" for very young children.** Include small prayer books, a children's Bible, a cross, a rosary, some crayons, a small note pad, or soft, quiet toys.

- **Make Sundays special.** Have a genuine day of rest – let your kids skip making beds or picking up laundry. Even if your job requires you to work on Sunday, make sure that you make time for prayer and relaxation. Take a walk together after church. Have a special meal with candles, a tablecloth or good dishes, and dessert! Avoid unnecessary shopping. Go for donuts or ice cream after Mass. Play a board game or read together. Visit relatives or friends.

● **Meet other parishioners.** Children are more engaged if they know people at church. Get to know other parishioners and linger for conversation after Mass. Children love running around with their friends while their parents chat. Attend church social functions to meet other parishioners. Encourage friendships with other parish children.

● **Get involved.** Church makes more sense to our children when we connect our prayer and our actions. When we serve our community, we teach our children the connection between *receiving* the Body of Christ at Mass and *becoming* the Body of Christ in the world.

● **Use your senses.** After Mass, light a votive candle together and say a prayer. Walk around and look at the stained glass windows, statues and stations of the cross. Take home some holy water and use it to bless your house or new bicycle or pet.

● **Honour mealtime.** The sacredness of family meals helps us understand the sacredness of the meal we share at Mass. Eat meals together as often as you can. Say grace before you eat. Make mealtime a time of sharing stories and enjoying each other rather than a time for discipline.

● **Relax!** While children do need to learn how to behave in formal settings, we must always remember that the Eucharist is a celebration!

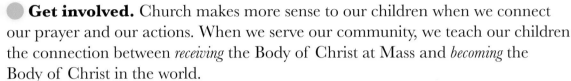

As we help our children learn to love and live the Sunday liturgy by participating more fully, we will find that we grow in our own understanding and appreciation of this wonderful gift.

Christine Way Skinner has been a parish catechist for 24 years. She has a Master of Divinity from Harvard Divinity School and is the author of *Jesus Invites Me to the Feast: My First Eucharist Journal* (Liguori). When she is not trying to find inclusive, compelling and creative ways to pass on the Catholic Church's tradition, Christine enjoys reading, art, gardening and trying to convince her husband, Michael, and their house full of children that they really do love playing board games with her.

Céleste Gagnon is a full-time illustrator and designer. Over the last 15 years, Céleste has worked on many projects, including books, magazines, novel covers, merchandise, clothing, and fabric design. She loves what she does and the variety of work that comes with being an illustrator. When she is not working, Céleste likes reading, hiking and enjoying nature with her husband and their two young children.